CO.
ROBBERS

A history of Policing in the town

The third of
four walks in the company of
'The Guy in the Kilt'

Ian Patterson

SECRET Shrewsbury

In memory of Arthur Drew, former constable
of Shrewsbury who took the author under
his wing and recounted some of the tales
contained herein.

*A special thanks to my son, John
for the illustrations.*

*The author also wishes to express his grateful
thanks to the Shrewsbury Tourist Board for
their support.*

Published by GET Publishing,
57 Queens Road, Bridgnorth, Shropshire WV15 5DG

Printed by Direct Imaging Ltd
1-3 Prince Road, Kings Norton, Birmingham B30 3HB

If you are expecting a technical text book, researching into the structures of buildings, exact dates; concise historical references – then you've got the wrong book. It's not Ian's way.

This History Walk is but one of four through the heart of this ancient town in the company of 'The Guy in the Kilt,' an instantly recognisable Town Guide, who has put his own individual stamp on this series of walks.

All four books are humorous, off-beat and tell the stories of Shrewsbury in a unique style – the way they were told to Ian as he walked the town's streets as a police officer since 1970.

'Secret Shrewsbury' is illustrated by Ian's son, John, and between them bring our beautiful town alive for both the armchair traveller and curious explorer alike.

Allow about an hour and a half for each walk except 'The River Round.' Although this can be walked in about the same time scale – it deserves to be a much more leisurely stroll; maybe even leaving the walk for a short time to explore other 'shuts and passages,' or calling in at one of the many quaint coffee shops for a well deserved break.

Enjoy.

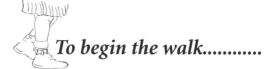

To begin the walk............

COPS AND ROBBERS

Stand to the front and right of the 16th century **Market Hall,** i.e. with your back to the Clive Statue and facing the Music Hall. At your feet, near to the base of the building, you'll see a depiction of the River Severn which surrounds Shrewsbury.

Welcome to the Saxon town of Scrobbsbyrig; a place chosen by Alfred the Great as one of his fortified places where markets, churches and the courts could flourish in safety. In fact, look at the way the river loops around the town: You don't have to be a military genius to drop a castle onto that narrow neck of land at the northern end of the town, to see why the location of this town was the perfect choice.

So, a place where law and order could be dispensed was right at the heart of the town's existence since it was formed sometime between 890 and 901 A.D. And this walk is going to concentrate on that – the growth of the law, ancient and modern, and its enforcement.

But why is the 'Guy in the Kilt' qualified to lead you through some of the little known tales about our beautiful town? Quite simply, he served two periods of duty here during his twenty five years police service; firstly as a constable under the tutelage of officers who'd been made privy to the stories in their turn by men who had policed in a different age; and secondly as a police inspector who walked the town daily until his retirement in 1988.

Well, we'd best get started:

Whereas policing 'proper' didn't start here until the 1 January, 1836 with the inaugural meeting of the Watch Committee, law and order wasn't a new concept. For instance, in 1006, King Ethelred the Unready visited the town where a hired assassin, a man called Porkhund, tried to take his life. He failed – but on every subsequent visit to the area, the king was to be guarded by twelve men, or Burgesses. [Wouldn't you just love to know the fate of Porkhund? I wish I knew, but I guess it was unpleasant.]

In 1280, three sergeants, one per ward were elected on the 1st Sunday after St Giles. [1st September is St Giles' Day.] These ancient wards were still the foot beats in the town when, 'The Guy in the Kilt' arrived here in 1970: Castle; Stone or English Bridge and Welsh or Frankwell; although they were now known as one, two and three beats.

We know the law was being enforced as early as 1384 – the court records showing us that the Night Watch were busily engaged in reporting offenders, like the Guild of St Alkmund, for leaving wood in the street overnight. This Night Watch consisted of townspeople taking their turn to guard the town on a rota basis, usually between the times when the gates were closed, [by 9 pm in summer,] and the ringing of the bell at St Julian's Church at 4 a.m.

The Market Hall we're now standing beside was converted for use as a magistrates' court early in the 20th century. And it has plenty of stories:

There was once a persistent criminal who used to steal cars. Sometimes he just left them when he wanted a different ride; sometimes he'd sell them. By the time he was twenty years old he had over thirty such convictions and was disqualified from driving until 2015 – nearly 50 years into the future. And he's due in court again.

A constable is arriving to give evidence in another case when the young man pulls up nearby, gets out of a car and, bold as brass, walks into court. The police officer is aghast; then realises that this is probably the easiest arrest he was ever likely to get.

The case is put back so the offender can be processed and have additional charges served on him and he's back before the magistrates that afternoon. In his defence, he tells the Bench that he's now got a job and needs a car; and anyway, the job is miles away and couldn't have got here today if he hadn't stolen one and driven here whilst disqualified.

The magistrates were none too pleased, – at the police, that is. "Unnecessary," was their choice of words; fined the offender five pounds on each offence – then had a whip-round on the Bench and paid his fines for him.

As we walk the streets, I should post a warning here: If it is a market day, [Thursday,] and you are a Welshman – it is still perfectly lawful for you to be killed in Shrewsbury: But only by a person wielding a sword – and only if he decapitates you. So, you're pretty safe.

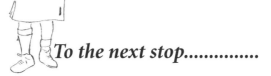*To the next stop...............*

Walk the way you are facing – toward the Music Hall with the Old Market Hall on your left, and turn right into Market Street. Take your first turning to the left at Talbot's Buildings, [the site of a police station in the 19th century and formerly a coaching inn and residence of the servants of the medieval Earls' of Shrewsbury,] into Swan Hill. Walk up the slight incline until the next road junction to your left, College Hill.

Stand facing the **Admiral Benbow pub.**

The pub itself used to be where the police did their drinking, but we are turning our attention to the well proportioned stone building immediately to the left of the Benbow. This was the main police station of the town for over seventy years from 1900, the Watch Committee having the foresight to buy the piece of land eighteen years earlier. And the name of the piece of ground: Scotland Yard. I kid you not.

To the right, above the ground floor windows, you'll see 'Weights and Measures Office' etched into the stonework. This is but one of the many and varied jobs given over to the police in the past: They were in charge of lodging houses, licensing; even the fire brigade. In the 1930's, Chief Inspector Falconbridge was killed whilst drilling his men in the use of ladders.

To the left of the old police station, there is a driveway leading to a yard – and another story:

There was a policeman stationed here nicknamed 'The Destroyer;' as in he was always on the look-out for subs. One of his money making exercises involved the collection of orders for fresh Christmas turkeys from all four shifts in the station; then telling his mate, who knew someone, who knew someone who had a lot of birds to get rid of. And for his bulk order, the Destroyer would get a freebee.

The birds arrive in the back of a scruffy white van. Only they arrive a day early; the 23 December, and they were frozen, not fresh. And it was unseasonably warm. Undeterred, the constable on station duty stacks the birds, each in their own cardboard box, into the garage in the yard – and tries to find the Destroyer who had the list of who had ordered what.

It was eight o' clock in the evening before the Destroyer arrived, to find fifty officers shuffling about nervously waiting for their Christmas dinners. Some were on duty and shouldn't be there; some were on nights and had to be back here in short order to start work – and, even in the pitch blackness of the yard, there was no disguising the water running under the garage door.

The Destroyer opens the doors, and with the only light available – his torch, he starts trying to find a bird to match the size of fowl ordered: "What was yours Jimmy? A ten-pounder…..Ah: Here it is…..." After the third, protracted search, the remaining officers were ready to lynch him. But the Destroyer was a quick thinker. He grabbed at the first bird he came to; guessed at the weight – and threw it out into the yard: "Twelve-pounder:" "Ten-pounder." It was working quite well, the blokes grabbing at the flying, half frozen birds

and sorting themselves out, until…..

Until it came to an incredibly slow, pipe sucking constable; Dirky, who could test the patience of a Saint as it took that long for him to formulate a sentence. "Fifteen-pounder," the cry came from the depths of the garage. "That might be….." SMACK! The huge bird came flying out of the darkness – and hit the unfortunate Dirky right between the eyes. Down he went; unconscious, but still gripping his pipe.

He came round in time for his dinner – but the turkey scam was never repeated.

To your left and about two hundred yards away, was the location for the headquarters of the Shropshire County Constabulary, but the building has been replaced by an old persons' home and bears no resemblance to its predecessor. The County Police had no jurisdiction within the Borough, but insisted on having a presence within the county town. Their officers, at least initially, must have been a rum lot. Excuse the pun – they lost nearly half of their 43 officers in the first year, [1839] to alcohol abuse and poaching.

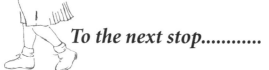

To the next stop............

Place your back toward the Admiral Benbow, and walk up the street opposite; College Hill. After about fifty yards, there is **a narrow alleyway on your left going down the side of the Music Hall**. Take that alley and stop where it widens.

We are now in **Coffee House Passage**, a very atmospheric place that doesn't take much to let your imagination run riot. We're here because there was a police station in the building immediately on our right between 1845 and 1853. The nine men of the Night Watch would turn out for duty in their top hats, [helmets replaced them in 1869,] with their wooden rattles, sabres and wooden truncheons to keep the town safe.

But "A policeman's lot is not a happy one;" it says so in the musical, Pirates of Penzance. And it wasn't. The constables worked between ten and twelve hours each day; seven days a week without ever having time off – and were expected to walk a minimum of twenty miles a shift. They earned the same as an unskilled, agricultural labourer, which meant they were on the breadline – and if they didn't find a break-in on their beat; even if it was through a window on an upper storey; they'd be charged with neglecting their duty: Hardly fair when they only had hand held lamps. Policemen were even denied the right to vote until 1887.

No surprise then: July 1846: Two fat geese were found wandering the town and taken to the police station here. The Town Crier broadcast the find, but when no one came forward to collect them, a local publican was asked to come to the station to bid for them. He did: But they'd gone!

When the police moved out, the premises became a brothel.

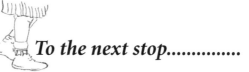

To the next stop...............

Continue down the passage and you will emerge into **The Square** just to the right of the main door of the Music Hall.

Stand just where you emerge.....

Your guide, Ian, did just that, one dark night in 1970. He'd followed the same route as we've just done from Swan Hill at the beginning of his night duty – and emerged into The Square – and into a world of trouble.

The Music Hall used to be the main source of entertainment for the young; only at ten

minutes past ten this particular Saturday night, the entertainment was going to be - me. I was surrounded by a couple of dozen, noisy and aggressive young men fuelled by alcohol and looking for 'sport.' The ring-leader was a huge man. Give him an axe and a hat with a couple of horns on it and he'd be straight off the Viking boats. He approached as his mates began to circle about me.

He looked down on my six foot frame and said, "We're Welsh and proud of it. Can you speak Welsh?"

'Don't say no,' I reasoned to myself: Instead I resorted to my broad Geordie accent. "Me la'! Ah canna even tark English, marra. No were I cum fraem." I might have said more – but to my new friends, it was all unintelligible gibberish.

After a few, very long seconds, the Viking began to laugh. "He's all right this one," he boomed. "Leave him alone."

Taking heart that I wasn't going to be pounded to death, I helped them on their way. "Aye; g'neet. Gan on wi ye; else ye miss yer bus haem. Yi'll ha' a lang wark thin."

But that's what policing was in the days when no help was coming your way: Without radios, you'd better be able to talk yourself out of trouble.

To the next stop.............

Turn to your right, [as if you'd just emerged from Coffee House Passage,] and walk up Princess Street. After the last building on your right; turn right and go up the incline, crossing the road and entering the cemetery of Old St Chad's Church. *For the disabled; you will have to use the roadway up the hill as the kerbs are high.* Keep to the main path through the cemetry until you get to the road at the other end. This is Belmont, [Beautiful Hill.]

Stand at the junction of the cemetery path and Belmont.

Just across the road is a terrace of rather fine houses. About ten yards to your left is the first of the terrace, slightly set back from the road itself and with stone gate posts; this is the **Judges' Lodgings:**

The Judges' Lodgings were built in 1701 for the High Court Judges visiting Shrewsbury during their 'circuit' of Assize Courts. These were the highest judges in the land – the 'Hanging Judges,' who with their black cap in hand held the power of life and death over

14

those who came before them.

Since medieval times, they've had to be protected. Armed police would accompany them to Old St Chad's, [the Lady Chapel of which still stands just to our left,] for the service which marked the beginning of the Assize sitting. I certainly spent many a long and cold night standing outside those gates wishing my life away – yet the Judges, the town and police had this sort of love – hate relationship. Back in the 1750s, the judges threatened to remove the Assizes from the town altogether, because they weren't being 'entertained' by the Borough in a proper manner. Of the police; even back in 1858, a judge warned his jury: "Be very cautious in accepting evidence from a police officer unless born out by responsible corroboration."

Fortunately, not all judges felt the same:

One of them was a war hero and very pro-police; so much so that every officer heaved a sigh of relief if he was sitting. He'd lost an arm during the 2nd World War and always balanced several volumes of heavy law books along the stiff, false limb.

Anyway, this one day he was sat listening to a defendant trying to argue that the police officers had stitched him up, when the judge's notorious temper got the better of him. He leaned forward, moved his spectacles to the end of his nose and peered over the top of them at the unfortunate criminal in the dock. The stare was icy enough to bring the man's diatribe to a faltering halt.

"Are you calling MY officers liars: These men of high repute and good character; men who put themselves in the face of danger every day for the good of society." His voice was rising like a volcano, until he half rose from his seat shouting, "You have the temerity to call them liars?"

The defence barrister was on his feet by now: "I apologise profusely for my client. I'm sure he didn't mean to cause offence….."

Fortunately, he stopped digging a hole for himself: One glare from on high was enough.

"Three months for the assault and three months for lying to this court about my officers. Take him down."

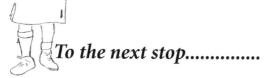

To the next stop...............

Turn left and walk passed the rear of Old St Chad's Church. Take the first

left, cross to the pavement on the other side of the street.
Stand at the entrance to the **Golden Cross Passage.**

Disabled or those with pushchairs etc. may wish to re-trace their route, turning right when you reach Princess Street again. The Golden Cross is but a few yards away on your left.

We've already said how difficult things were, especially for those early constables. Maybe the licensees of public houses just wanted to help, [or bribe,] the guardians of the peace – but they certainly used to leave a drink out for the men on duty.

One such was Constable Walkerdine. He was a policeman in the town just after the 2nd World War and unfortunately liked a drop of beer just a little too much. He was drunk every night by midnight, thanks to the pints of beer left in this, and other, passageways. His wife, Marion, was a God-send. She knew if he lost his job, they lost their house and goodness knows where the money would come from then. So, she'd meet him in the Golden Cross Passage at midnight; walk him home – then don his uniform; pop on his helmet and walk the streets for the rest of the night. And they were never discovered.

Even before the 2nd World War, the ability to get a drink at any time was legendary. A new Chief Constable was appointed for Shropshire, and decides he would try and catch out his men – make an impression – before they got to know him. So, off he goes in mufti; finds a constable and asks him, "Can you get me a drink officer? It's an awful hot day and I'm parched dry."

"I'm sorry sir," the constable replied. "It's outside of the licensing hours."

"Surely, you can get us a drink," insisted the stranger; so the policeman takes him to the back door of a nearby public house and raps loudly on the door. When both men are standing with drinks in hand, the stranger asks, "What would you say if your sergeant appeared now?"

The constable replied without hesitation. "Well, sur. I would say I'm having a drink at the invitation of the new Chief Constable."

Not so stupid…..

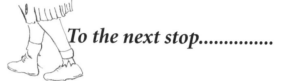

To the next stop...............

Continue down the alley until you reach the end. Turn right onto High Street and walk to the next junction. This will be **Milk Street.**

Stand at the junction looking in the direction of the Old Post Office Inn some ten yards to your right.

The building to the left of the inn, more or less directly opposite us, is the site of the Shearman's Hall – and the area in which we're standing, the only place in town where the Riot Act has been read.

Basically, toward the end of the 16th century, 500 people turned out to protest, for and against, the demands of the Puritans to have an oak sapling removed from the door to the Guild of the Shearmen. That particular Act of Parliament is quite simplistic: If you're still here in an hour – we'll kill you.

Turn to your left and look at St Julian's Church.

It was here in 1265, that Thomas, servant of Henry Borey, a clerk in Shrewsbury, fled for sanctuary after killing a man in a tavern brawl. As with other felons of the time, Thomas could claim sanctuary within the church for up to forty days before having to face arrest and the courts.

But back to the early 1970s and the saga of Winky Heron, a Gypsy man who had one glass eye – hence the name. His proper name was Kenny, and if Kenny was in a fight – which he was, often, invariably his eye would be knocked out of the socket. He'd pick it up, breathe on it; polish it on his jumper and push it back in.

View from St. Julian's Steps

It was a holiday weekend and Winky had certainly enjoyed himself. He'd been locked up twice already – both times for assaulting a police officer, but he was such a nuisance in the cells – the confinement sending him crazy; he was always given bail.

And here was I, just where we are now; clock-watching, just another ten minutes and I could go home, when Kenny Heron appeared in front of me. "Good evening, Mr Heron," I said pleasantly knowing that you didn't use his nickname which acted as a trigger for a fight.

But Kenny was having none of it. I was greeted by a whole lot of words ending with 'ing.'

"I'm not locking you up, so you're wasting your time," I said, turning to go.

He grabbed my arm, put himself in front of me and raised his fists.

"Mr Heron: There is no way….." I began to reason with him – and I have to admit I never saw it coming. Somewhere from behind me came a well-dressed man in a suit and carrying an umbrella. Without breaking step, he reversed the brolly and hit Winky so hard with the bone handle, it felled the old Gypsy: Spark out in the road.

"That'll teach him," said the concerned citizen in a suit as he kept walking.

I might have walked off as well – but Kenny's eye had popped out and was lying in the gutter. No one at the station was pleased to have him back, but the sergeant accepted my apologies and locked him up for the night.

I learned later, that when it came time to bail him out in the early hours, some idiot constable had called him Winky as he handed back the glass eye. The old Gypsy went wild, throwing the eye at the offender. Fortunately it missed – and it took three constables twenty minutes to find it again, by which time Kenny had calmed down sufficiently to be allowed to leave.

To the next stop...............

Cross the road in front of St Julian's;

turn right and with the church now on your left; walk to the **top of Wyle Cop**. **Stand** on the pavement where it widens and look across the road at **The Lion Hotel.**

For the last thousand years, the Wyle Cop has probably been the most violent place in Shrewsbury. In 1074 A.D. Bloudy Jack, Shrewsbury's own serial killer, had his head placed on a pole just where we're now standing. He was guilty all right – he'd kept all the fingers and toes of his female victims; and as it was the policy of the time to execute the offender within the view of the victims house, at least one of the girls he raped and murdered, must have lived close by.

It was a Saturday night in the January of 1596 when Richard Twisse murdered an Oswestry man just outside the Lion Hotel. Richard rode off and the 'hue and cry' was raised to catch him. It's something akin to a posse you see in the Wild West films; the sanctuary being offered by St Julian's just a few yards away, having been abolished by Henry V111 when he reformed the church in England: [Education, hospitals and welfare all disappeared during the break with Rome.]

But all that was as naught compared to what

the area was like when the Navigators arrived in the town to build the canals and railways. In fact, by 1879, it was too dangerous to send a single constable down the Cop to Coleham. It was seen as legitimate sport to throw a policeman into a coal fire, hit them with an axe or shoot at them. On one occasion, a licensee saved the life of a constable by locking him in the cellar of his pub until the danger had passed.

It was at 11pm on a November night in 1847 – two years before it was deemed too dangerous to patrol the Wyle Cop - and the navvies are drinking in town. Fights are breaking out everywhere. Constable Farmer is punched in the eye trying to stop twelve men killing one another. He arrests his attacker, but he's now got a problem. Several more Irish arrive and attack him with knives. He beats them off with his truncheon, but loses his prisoner. Later, he sees the man again on the Cop and grabs him once more.

Just at that moment, the constable's colleague, Pc Finch, is not fifty yards away outside the Unicorn pub having yet more trouble with the drunken Irish. Things got a whole lot worse when the English navvies, just as drunk, arrive to 'help' and are threatened with being thrown into 'the Big Say,' as the Irish called the Severn.

More English: More Irish: The fight grows, one labourer taking off his wooden leg and wading in with it. I reckon the two cops must have decided to stick to the one prisoner – and left the rest to it. But that's the way it was.

It hadn't changed much by my time policing

the town – but just by a way of a change from violence; one little story I'm particularly fond of.

It concerns, in the first instance, the narrow alley, on the same side as the Lion Hotel, and slightly to our right.

Night shift can get a bit cold, wet and lonely. And certainly during my earlier years walking the beat; you were in serious trouble if you were found to be off your appointed area – and that included being on the wrong side of the street.

But sometimes you took a chance to have a chat; sort of break the monotony of the early hours – and one such night, I was standing here talking with a friend, Don. It was three in the morning and cold, so we had our heavy great coats on. As we spoke, a great commotion could be heard coming toward us: Totally alien sounds.

Then, within seconds, the biggest rat you've ever seen came into view, running for its life down the alleyway opposite. It was pursued by a cat, a mere six inches off its tail, and the rat swivelled in mid air as it ran, clawing wildly at its tormentor. But the cat wasn't going to be put off. The battle got closer and closer, but fortunately was still taking place over there.

Don hated rats – ever since he'd heard of a horde of them coming up Wyle Cop from the river; so many they'd filled the road; several feet deep with their diseased, furry bodies and actually forced a constable to abandon his pedal cycle and climb onto a window sill to let them pass. So, Don thought he'd help the cat. "Let's put our torches on," he said. "Cat'll see better."

So, like a couple of idiots, we did, catching the rat in beams of light which would have graced any drama about 2nd World War bombers. The rat turned without breaking stride – and ran straight across the road at us; the cat still immediately behind. It never deviated from the torch beam.

Now; I hate rats as much as the next man – and was a bit quicker on the uptake than Don. I switched my torch off.

He didn't. The rat ran at his light; went up his leg; up his sleeve; onto his shoulder – the cat followed. The rat leapt from his shoulder for the wall behind you and somehow flattened itself into a hole you couldn't get your car keys into.

Don's screams joined those of the rat and cat – only his went on and on and on as the cat settled down for a long wait. But we were off; frightened in equal measure by the rat and the probable arrival of our equally fearsome sergeant to investigate the noise in his town.

To the next stop...............

Re-trace your steps toward St Julian's Church. Just before you reach the church, turn right up the steps at the side of the graveyard. Follow the narrow passageway of St Julian's Shut until it widens out into **St. Alkmund's Square.**

Walk past the church; then stand in the churchyard, [i.e. to the right,] with your back to the building.

For the Disabled or those with pushchairs, access to St Alkmund's Square will have to be via Dogpole. Turn left at the junction; the one opposite the Lion, and continue up the street until you come to the first alleyway on your left. You can't miss it – Dogpole House juts out across the public footpath, narrowing it considerably. Go down the alley and through the bollards – there is enough room for a wheelchair; and bear right through the small square. St Alkmund's Church is now on your left. Go past the church and enter the churchyard. Make sure your back is to the building.

St Alkmund's Square, all about this ancient church, is the centre of Saxon Shrewsbury. Animals were bought and sold just where we're standing; taken the few yards to **Butcher Row,** [directly in front of you and **to the left of the**

Prince Rupert Hotel,] for slaughter in the street**.**

The Abbot's House, directly facing the hotel, dates from the mid-late 1450s with the ground floor being used as shops; mainly butchers. The present day windows would have been covered by shutters, raised at night for security. However, the

court records show that the Night Watch was particularly vigilant as vagrants, drunks and the poor would let the shutters down – not to steal necessarily, but to get somewhere dry to sleep. It mattered not: They were appearing in court regularly.

By the 1850s **The Abbot's House** had become a notorious tenement building; no doubt because of the tremendous influx of the navigators; 'navvies;' both English and Irish, who arrived in the town to construct the railways and canal.

In fact, as early as the 1830s, there were eleven beer houses in the square about us to meet the demand, leading the local vicar's wife to begin the local Temperance League. She was probably not as successful as she'd wish to be, as by 1879 there were 191 licensed premises in Shrewsbury attracting the attention of the Salvation Army. Things were so bad, that wherever the 'Sally' went, they had to be accompanied by the police.

To the next stop..........

Turn to your right and face down Church Street:

In my early years in Shrewsbury, there is an unhappy story which occurred just outside the Loggerheads public house, in **Church Street.** It is 11 p.m. and there's a disturbance outside the pub. Fortunately, two patrolling constables hear the noise and arrive in double-quick time to find one youth on the ground with another astride him going through his pockets.

The offender runs off chased by one of the officers, whilst the other helps the attacked man to his feet. He's battered and shaken, but says he's okay and if he hurries he can still catch the last bus home.

The constable is not so sure. This is a case of robbery; he needs a statement and….. But just at that moment he hears the sound of a fight coming from off to our right. The chasing constable has caught the robber. No more thinking time: The caring constable leaves his witness with a, "Wait there," and rushes off to help.

The assaulted man is now in a dilemma: Wait for the policeman to come back – or go for his bus? He runs for the bus: Wrong choice.

Two huge detectives had just left the Loggerheads. [I'm six feet tall and at the time was the smallest bloke on the shift; so these detectives were massive.] They 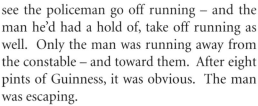 see the policeman go off running – and the man he'd had a hold of, take off running as well. Only the man was running away from the constable – and toward them. After eight pints of Guinness, it was obvious. The man was escaping.

The victim-cum-witness was running flat out, thoughts only of making it to the bus stop before the bus arrived. It was a long walk home.

The two detectives move aside to let the

runner come between them; then at the last moment, came back together; shoulder to shoulder. Their hands never came out of their pockets, but they hit the lad so hard, that all his money was knocked from his pockets. The coins fell tinkling to the pavement. He joined them a split second later. He was flattened: Didn't know if it was night or morning.

The two detectives, feeling pretty pleased with themselves, took an arm each and dragged the unfortunate back to the two uniformed constables around the corner. They found them disconsolate: The robber had fled – and realised immediately, not only did they have no prisoner, but now they had an unconscious witness as well.

"Here's your prisoner, son," said the two burly men dropping the unconscious form at their feet – and left.

"But….."

"No need for thanks," said one of the unhurried, retreating backs. "Glad to be of help."

One of the uniforms hits on a good idea just as the man starts to come around.

"What happened," he asked?

"You were mugged son," said the quick thinking cop. "Come on; we'll give you a hand."

So off they trotted to the police station where they cleaned the witness up and gave him a pot of tea whilst the offence of robbery was recorded and a statement taken. On the question of the description of his assailants, the witness was a bit vague – but so much the better in the circumstances. At the end of it all, the constables gave the young man his taxi fare home.

The young man couldn't thank the officers enough as they escorted him to the door: Handshakes all round. Just then, two imposing figures appeared out of the night, brushed passed the little group and disappeared toward the C.I.D. office.

"You know," said the lad. "I could swear those robbers were a bit like those two."

"Nah! They're detectives."

"Ah well: Thanks for all your kindness."

To the next stop...............

Continue along Church Street with the Loggerheads pub, an early brick built building dating from 1665, on your right. When you get to the end, cross straight over St Mary's Street.

Stand on the pavement looking toward the front door of the church under the tower. There is no need to approach the church.

Back in 1589, St Mary's Street; the one in front of the church, was no more than an open sewer, with the pavement just as narrow as it is now. Just this side of the gate into the churchyard in

front of the tower, was a 'mounting block,' to enable people to get onto their horses more easily. And the block took up even more of the pavement, so that only one person at a time could pass.

On Friday, 8 March, Richard Prynce, a lawyer of Whitehall, (a mansion he'd built out of stone he'd stolen from the Abbey – then painted it white to disguise what he'd done*), was attending the funeral of a notable personage at the church. I suspect Richard wasn't universally popular – because Robert Ireland, a merchant with serious money and a mansion which still stands on the High Street; refused to give precedence to Prynce as they both arrived at the narrow point together. Both were going to the funeral; both had no intention of stepping into the quagmire – and both would not give an inch. It came to blows; then Ireland stabbed Prynce. Their servants joined in and a right good melee developed before the service had even begun. Later, Ireland appeared before the court and was fined six shillings and eight pence for 'a blood.'

*In fairness to Mr Prynce, he always claimed that he painted the stone of his 'Whitehall' to protect it from the elements.

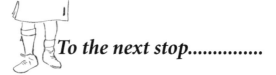 *To the next stop..............*

Keep the church on your left, walk along the pavement down St Mary's Square, keeping to the nearside of the road. Follow the footpath around to the rear of the church.

For the Disabled or those with pushchairs the kerbs are high, so you'll have to stay on the roadway. Fortunately, vehicular traffic isn't too heavy.

At the rear of the church; **The Old Nurses Home** is now found directly in front of you, with the **Old Royal Salop Infirmary,** [RSI] on your right. **Between the two is an entrance**  to parking spaces beneath the Old Nurses Home. **Stand** with your back to the side wall of the RSI looking at the Nurses home. There are now car parking spaces beneath the current, re-furbished building. This was a location which loomed large in the life of a uniformed constable, certainly until the early 1970s.

Not only was the mortuary here but the invaluable **'stoke-hole' under the Nurses Home.** The greedy furnace had to be fed very frequently in order for the hospital to function, which meant the night stoker never got any rest – unless the cops came in to help out. He could get his head down for a while confident in the knowledge that the 'boys in blue' would stoke the fires for him – and deplete his stocks of tea and coffee. But it was seen as a fair trade by all concerned – for constables on foot patrol will always find a place to shelter from the elements. However, there is a problem: If you've been warm and dry – and it's been raining – how do you convince your sergeant you haven't been neglecting your duty? Answer: You find a broken down pipe and stand under it until your coat is wet enough to fool him.

Unfortunately, one constable thought he'd be clever and left his coat outside, strategically positioned to catch the rain. In this way, he calculated he could stay in the warm for an extra three minutes. He eventually returned to the station full of confidence that his trick had worked – only the sergeant went ballistic at him, threatening all sorts of dire consequences if he continued to tell lies about where he'd been. He gave in: "How did you know, sergeant," he asked?

"Take a look at your helmet, son."

The constable did. It was as dry as a bone.

"Next time, leave it outside with your coat," said the wise old officer who'd done it all; seen it all before.

To the next stop............

Return to the roadway at the rear of St Mary's Church. Turn right and continue to walk around the church; i.e. keep it on your left. Walk for a further fifty yards.

St**and,** just before you get to the **Yorkshire House pub.**

The disabled or those with pushchairs will have to remain on the road.

The Yorkshire House used to be the 'druggies' pub back in the late sixties and early seventies – and is the scene of an amusing story.

The licensee of the Yorkshire House phoned the police station at lunchtime one day to ask for help; something unusual it itself. But there was a lady in his pub refusing to leave – and "Oh: By the way: She's naked."

Police cars speed to the scene, the officers no doubt expecting a bit of light relief. They were to be disappointed. If the lady in question was undoubtedly naked, she was undoubtedly huge:  Grotesquely so – and uncooperative with it. She drew more attention to herself by continually shouting, "It's me burf-day."

There weren't enough constables on duty to get her into a vehicle without her agreement – and she'd have none of it. Not that it mattered – we didn't have a big enough vehicle she'd fit into anyway.

So, it was time for compromise. We'd all sing one chorus of 'happy birthday,' if she'd go straight home afterwards. And that's what happened – even though she had a half a mile to walk right through the centre of town – naked.

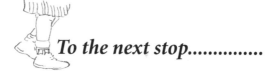

To the next stop...............

Look at the building to the right of the Yorkshire House. It is an old timber framed building with a narrow passage to the right which actually goes through the house itself. To get an idea of what conditions used to be like in the town back in medieval times, walk through the passage; [it's called Little Shut and is a public right of way,] through the yard beyond, then plunge once more into the continuation of the shut, [alleyway] directly opposite. You'll emerge in Castle Street. Cross the road and turn right. **Walk down Castle Street** for about fifty yards and **turn left into Castle Court.**

Stand in the entrance to the courtyard. There is no need to go right in and the residents have asked for their privacy to be respected.

For the Disabled or those with pushchairs, I'm afraid there is no option but to go back the way you came, until you get to the rear of the church and turn left. Continue on the roadway until you get to Castle Street. Cross the road at the pedestrian lights; turn right and after about fifty yards, Castle Court is on your left.

To the right of Castle Court is a building with a set of steps leading up to a doorway. This was the town gaol and House of Correction from 1704-5 for about a hundred years. The cells were below ground level and were "Wretched in accommodation and a school of vice." Even the gaoler brewed his own alcohol – and sold it to the prisoners.

Those of you who have read, or taken, the Ghost Walk, will know that a police constable hung himself in there – and changed his mind half way through the act; his hands tearing at the noose: But one story I particularly like, is that of Jeremiah Upton who was condemned to death for murdering his wife in 1741. Whilst waiting for the sentence to be carried out, he ordered a coffin to be made for him 'complete with brass nails,' and valued at twelve shillings and six pence. It was duly delivered – but Jeremiah had friends who managed to get his sentence reduced to twenty years transportation. The unwanted coffin was put to good use. He dressed someone up in a white sheet and had him lie in the coffin; then put 'his body' on show charging people a penny a time to view the 'corpse.'

And off he went to the colonies without paying the coffin maker. Twenty one years later, he's back in Shrewsbury having completed his sentence – and being pursued by Edward Leake, the coffin maker, for payment.

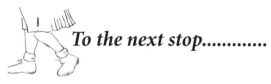

To the next stop............

Return to Castle Street and turn right. Keep on the right hand pavement and walk back to **The Cross** at the top of **Pride Hill. Stand** at **The Cross**.

We are now at one of the principal execution sites in Shrewsbury where David, the last 'real' Prince of Wales was hung, drawn and quartered and where the body of Harry Hotspur, leader of the rebellion in 1403 was dismembered and his adherents killed. It was also perfectly normal for an offender to be put to death in a place which could be seen from the deceased's home or on one of the main routes into the town.

As you look down the pedestrianized **Pride Hill,** on your right you will see the entrance to an old, now unused, shut called **70 Steps.**

Immediately to the right of that opening, the building which stands there now used to be called, **'The Disorderly House,'** which must give us some idea what the pub was like.

This is a story from the early 1970s – before pedestrianization, when there was a narrow pavement outside The Disorderly House to separate those on foot from the heavy, vehicular traffic.

Jimmy the Frog was the ugliest police constable you'd ever see. His facial expression wasn't helped by an ill-fitting wig - which he steadfastly refused to admit the existence of. The hair-piece was so bad that when he put his helmet  on, or took it off, he had to hold it in place with the other hand. And Jimmy was as lazy as he was ugly. He would neither arrest, nor report, anyone for any offence whatsoever.

It fell to me to take him to task; an odious duty but made necessary by an incident which had occurred outside the Disorderly House on the previous week of night duty. A couple of constables had responded to a call about a drunk asleep in the shop doorway of the premises and as they tried to rouse him, unsuccessfully, they realized they'd been presented with a chance to make The Frog do some work. They'd seen him walking in their direction and calculated he'd pass this very spot within a couple of minutes. So they pulled the drunk out of the doorway and spread him out over the pavement: Then hid.

Jimmy appeared on cue, patrolling at the regulation, slow pace. He walked toward the trap – only when he got to the drunk, he didn't even break stride. He stepped over the unconscious form – and kept walking.

So: Time for action: Time for some man-management: "Out there this afternoon," I said in a strident voice. "And get me an offence: Any offence, I don't care….."

Three hours later and I'm walking down the main street, when the ungainly constable crosses the road; salutes; then grins at me. "Sir," he begins. "I've been up and down the High Street for hours and I've only found one offence."

"Good man," I reply. My pep talk had worked. I must be good at this man management job. "What is it?"

"It's an expired tax disc on a vehicle, sir."

"Well done. You see; you can do it if you keep your eyes peeled. Have you reported the owner?"

"No, sir: I thought I'd better speak to you first."

"And why is that," I ask not able to disguise my exasperation?

"Well: It's your car."

To the next stop...............

Carry on down Pride Hill until the High Street joins it from the left. The road sweeps away around to the left and as it does so, a footpath down Roushill is to be found on your right. Go down **Roushill** until the bank begins to steepen. **Stand** at the top of the bank.

Imagine you are a policeman. It's a warm day, blue skies and God is in His heaven. Then a report is received: "There's a body lying by the wall in Roushill." An unpleasant task - but off you go to investigate; ending up here. And true enough, there's a body.

Unfortunately, on the day in question, the officer who ended up here was Constable 'Ticker' Purvis. Ticker says he has a bad heart and can't do anything energetic or get too excited – not that anyone believed him; so it had taken him a while to wander his way into Roushill. There's definitely a body – he can see that from ten yards away – so there's no sense in walking down the bank as he'll have to come back up. And anyway; Ticker doesn't like dead bodies. He gets a message back to the police station that the death is suspicious – in that way; C.I.D. have to attend – and he'd be on his way.

He hangs around, well away from the deceased and after a fairly lengthy delay Detective Sergeant Charlie Whitelaw turns up. He'd lost the toss apparently. Only Charlie didn't like dead bodies either, so he gets no closer than the constable. "We'll wait for the police surgeon to come and pronounce life extinct," says the sergeant to Ticker.

In due course, a young stand-in police surgeon attends. By this time there's quite a crowd gathered and old Ticker is puffing and panting trying to keep them back. Only the doctor doesn't like dead bodies either. He stops twenty yards away, wrinkles his nose in disgust and states: "He's dead: Over to you sergeant."

"Constable Purvis," says the sergeant. "Go search the deceased's pockets. Find out who he is so we can inform the next-of-kin."

Grumbling under his breath about 'defective sergeants,' Ticker heads over to the corpse, bends down and with his fingertips, starts to gently rifle the man's pockets. He'd barely withdrawn the wallet when the 'corpse' jumps up shouting that he's being robbed; snatches back the wallet – and runs off.

Couldn't have done Ticker's ticker much good – but he hadn't lost his sense of humour. The station records are endorsed: 'Dead – but still breathing.'

To the next stop................

Carry on down Roushill Bank and take the first turning on your left. Walk the short distance until you reach the **Mardol**; the road which runs right to left in front of you.

Stand on the pavement at the junction. This has been a most necessary location for police officers to stand whilst on night duty: You can see all the action as the public houses disgorge their customers.

The **Mardol** or the 'Devil's Boundary,' has always been a violent place throughout its history of being a port and a 'red light' district. It was no different in the 1970s:

Shrewsbury once boasted a professional boxer as one of its citizens: A young man who had the world at his feet – if he did but know it. He was rumoured to be a contender – a Champion of the World in waiting. Unfortunately, he liked his drink a little too much and frequently ended up in gutter fights here in the Mardol.

And one night; he's just here, challenging everyone coming out of the pubs to a fight.

Being the new boy in Shrewsbury, I had no idea who he was; nor heard of his reputation. And my colleagues were happy enough for me to put my best foot forward to see 'what I was made of.'

Never one to back down, I approached the boxer. "Now then: Why don't you….."

He took a swing at me and missed by a country mile. Then again: Third swing – this time he put so much into it, that he fell over; dead drunk at my feet. The rest was easy.

An embarrassing arrest – but at least I'd earned my 'spurs:' - the guys could trust me. But the story grew and grew – and before I knew it, I had my nickname: 'Floyd:' [After the former World Heavyweight Champion.]

But the boxer was a nice guy. Later, when we're bailing him out at five in the morning, I ask him why he drinks so much.

"I likes it when I'm drinkin' it," he replied. "But when it's gone; it don't agree with me at all."

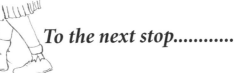

To the next stop............

Turn to your left and continue up the Mardol until you come to **Mardol Head.**

Stand in the vicinity of the **Darwin Gate sculpture.**

Mardol Head was also known as Lee Stalls back in the 1200s and was the location for many metal and goldsmiths and pawn shops. Really, most of the work was done in silver. We know that a 'Juliana of Ardeston' made a complaint against William the Goldsmith when he failed to return a bell she'd left as a security with him for the loan of two shillings.

Standing at the top of the rowdy Mardol, it was an ideal location to site a police pillar. In the days before radios, the only way a patrolling constable could be contacted was by illuminating the blue, flashing light of a police box or pillar. That is, if he was required urgently; otherwise the constable would make 'points.'

There were other pillars near the Royal Salop Infirmary in St Mary's Place and at both the English and Welsh Bridges. The police boxes – the 'Doctor Who' type – were reserved for the more out-of-town locations such as Frankwell, [near Darwin's house,] Castlefields and Abbey Foregate, near the Shirehall.

The police point system meant that when each officer paraded for duty, he'd be given a list of places where he HAD to be at a certain time. If it was three p.m. for instance; you'd be expected to be there at 2.55 and remain there until 3.05. There were no excuses for not making a point – and 'points' were often used as punishment.

For instance, a pigeon is handed in at the police station: Not any old pigeon, but a racing bird, no less, with a ring on one of its very valuable legs. A call to someone 'in the know,' revealed that this particular feathery friend was a prize winner; the father of many a champion – and that it had got lost during a race three days earlier somewhere 'up north.' The owner had been contacted and was already hastening toward us from afar.

To keep the thing safe, I thought it would be a good idea to put it in the stray dog pound out the back. A dark kennel would be just the thing to reduce its stress and aid its recovery. So that's what happened.

By 5 p.m. I was heading for tea when a bedraggled dog was being left with another hapless constable who had better things to do. He did the paperwork before pushing the half-starved beast into the pound: No dog food – it wasn't provided and he had no intention of handing over his cheese sarnies to it.

And that was that – until the pigeon owner turned up, pleased as punch that his prized bird had been found and was in safe hands. He was so excited – but it didn't last long. He left distressed; the pigeon somehow had found a hole in the wire mesh and flown off. It must have been a very small hole – what with the hundred's of feathers it left behind.

But the scruffy hound didn't seem to mind. It was licking its lips and grinning hugely.

The punishment: Half hourly points – which in effect meant you had but twenty minutes to get to the appointed place to be met by your sergeant. So, the offending officers – the one who hadn't fed the dog and the Pigeon Boy who'd stuck it in the kennel – passed one another at a near trot without the oxygen necessary for small talk. Repeat for eight hours.

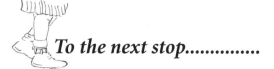

To the next stop...............

Cross directly over the road and enter **Gullet Passage. Stand about** five yards before the steps at the far end.

Gullet Passage comes from the 'Middle English' speech 'golate,' meaning stream. It was the natural outflow from the Ice Age kettle hole that was The Square, which over the centuries had filled with water – and the effluent shoved into it by the people of the town. From Gullet Passage, the foul stream would make its way to marshy ground by the Welsh Bridge, and eventually into the river.

The public house we now have in the alley is called the 'Hole in the Wall.' It was a debtors' prison at one time; perhaps even a place where lepers would be fed – but without the non-affected person coming into contact with them. In order to remain safe; make a hole in the wall and fit a revolving tray: Put food in – and swivel the tray so the food disappears into the darkness on the other side. No contact. Back in 1504, the pub was called 'The Gullet;' and a place to which the Drapers' Guild would go to drink.

In 1838, the fledgling Borough Police had an office in the passage. In the basement, you'd find the cells. The ground floor was the actual police station and office for weights and measures etc. whilst a policeman lived in the upper storey.

It was in this passage, that I first met Gary Cooper. Only this Gary wasn't a film star – just a nuisance criminal whose mouth got him into more trouble than enough. It was just after 10 p.m. and in another hour I could go home – and then, there was Gary, hurtling down the steps from The Square and into my arms. "Thank God I've found you," he says. "Lock me up for the night will you?"

"No!"

"Please: There's a gang of Brummie villains in town looking to do my legs."

"Why?"

"A misunderstanding, that's all, constable. But they're here all right and not going until they do me. Lock me up."

"No chance."

"Please….."

"Look: The only way I'll lock you up is if you'll put the shop windows in under the Market Hall." That would make him understand I wasn't going to be made a mug of: Imagine presenting him to the sergeant saying, "He wants….." Anyway, my refusal got rid of him.

Five minutes later I could hear a strange sound coming from Market Street; an irregular thump – thump: I about turn and go to investigate. It was Gary, swinging a canvas knapsack and striking it against a plate glass window. The glass would shudder and shake, but hadn't yet broke. He managed two further swipes before I got to him.

"Pack it in officer," he said, trying to shake me off and grab his bag back. "I've not broken it yet."

"And you're not going to. If this window breaks, the shards could cut you in two."

"Lock me up then."

But I had too much fear of my sergeant, so had to come up with a better idea. "Don't worry. I'll make sure the Brummies won't find you in a hurry." Within minutes, I was loading my 'prisoner' into the back of a police car. Initially, he was quite excited at being safe and happily looking forward to the short ride to a warm cell. His consternation grew as the town centre fell far behind us, and when we deposited him somewhere near Wales, I was as popular as the Brummie Gangsters. You can tell these things - from the amount of colourful language my driver and I were treated to as we wished him a good – and safe – night.

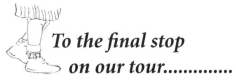

To the final stop on our tour.............

Carry on up the steps at the end of Gullet Passage and you will emerge into **The Square** with the **Old Market Hall**, once a **Magistrates' Court**, directly in front of you. **Stand** by the old court.

For the Disabled or those with pushchairs, you will have to go back the way you came. Turn right as you emerge onto the main thoroughfare; take your first right into High Street and first right again into The Square.

I think it only right and proper to bring this tour to an end with a story from yesteryear.

Now; nicknames were common – I think we've seen a few examples as we've heard our tales today: But none can ever compare with that of the, 'Policeman Jockey.' In the November of 1880, there was to be a horse race meeting in Shrewsbury and the six officers delegated to attend were given horses and told to parade in The Square. The superintendent carried out his inspection of his men and horses under the gaze of the townspeople. He checked that the bridles and boots were clean – and that all his men were dressed correctly in great coats, helmets and carried their long truncheons. Once he was satisfied, the men all rode off to Kingsland where the race was to be held. One constable, Dick Williams, was positioned near the starting gate in time for the first race of the afternoon.

The favourite for the race was being ridden by the famous 19th century jockey, Fred

Archer, also known as 'the Tinman,' for some reason which escapes me. But Fred had 246 wins already that season and was unbeatable. A lot of money was on him.

The flag drops and they're off. Unfortunately for Constable Williams, his horse decides to join in – and takes off after the rest of the field. He's dressed for a cold winter's day – not in racing silks. He's carrying a truncheon; not a whip – but nothing slows his horse down. He can't control it and just hangs on for grim death. He passes one horse after another – despite hauling on the reins. The final furlong: Dick is still in the saddle; still hanging on – but his horse is now neck and neck with the Tinman.

The professional jockey is worried. He should be cantering in – but there he is flying toward the line – only he's got a police horse alongside with its rider giving it "Whoa;" arms and legs all over the place. The crowd is going wild – despite their money being on the Tinman.

Fortunately, the professional came through – by a short neck. No doubt he heaved a sigh of relief which would be nearly as loud as the policeman's.

Of the fate of 'The Policeman Jockey' at the hands of his superintendent; nothing is recorded.

These and many more stories can be found in Ian's book: **The Thick Blue Line.**